Sous Vide Cookbook 2021-2022

The Ultimate Guide For Beginners With Amazing and Mouthwatering Recipes for Effortless Everyday Cooking.

Flavie Johnson

Furthermore, the transmission, duplication, or reproduction of any of the following work including specific information will be considered an illegal act irrespective of if it is done electronically or in print. This extends to creating a secondary or tertiary copy of the work or a recorded copy and is only allowed with the express written consent from the Publisher. All additional right reserved.

The information in the following pages is broadly considered a truthful and accurate account of facts and as such, any inattention, use, or misuse of the information in question by the reader will render any resulting actions solely under their purview. There are no scenarios in which the publisher or the original author of this work can be in any fashion deemed liable for any hardship or damages that may befall them after undertaking information described herein.

Additionally, the information in the following pages is intended only for informational purposes and should thus be thought of as universal. As befitting its nature, it is presented without assurance regarding its prolonged validity or interim quality. Trademarks that are mentioned are done without written consent and can in no way be considered an endorsement from the trademark holder.

Table of Contents

BREAKFAST

Coconut Berry Mix

Preparation time: 10 minutes

Cooking time: 20 minutes

Servings: 2

Ingredients:

2 tablespoons sugar

½ teaspoon vanilla extract

Juice of 1 lemon

1 cup blackberries

1 cup heavy cream

2 tablespoons coconut flakes

Directions:

In a bowl mix the berries with the cream and the other ingredients, toss, divide in canning jars, put the lid on, introduce in your sous vide machine and cook at 147 degrees F for 20 minutes.

Divide into bowls and serve for breakfast.

Nutrition: calories 152 fat 3 fiber 3 carbs 6 protein 4

Parmesan Eggs

Preparation time: 10 minutes

Cooking time: 35 minutes

Servings: 4

Ingredients:

½ cup parmesan, grated

Salt and black pepper to the taste

2 scallions, chopped

4 eggs

2 tablespoons chives, chopped

½ teaspoon sweet paprika

½ teaspoon cumin, ground

Directions:

Crack each egg in a sous vide bag, season with the chives, paprika and the other ingredients, seal the bags, submerge in the water oven and cook at 150 degrees F for 35 minutes.

Divide between plates and serve for breakfast.

Nutrition: calories 162 fat 3 fiber 6 carbs 12 protein 5

Scrambled Eggs

Preparation time: 10 minutes

Cooking time: 30 minutes

Servings: 2

Ingredients:

> teaspoon cumin, ground
>
> Salt and black pepper to the taste
>
> 1 tablespoon chives, chopped
>
> 4 eggs, whisked
>
> ½ teaspoon rosemary, dried
>
> ½ teaspoon sweet paprika
>
> ½ teaspoon chili powder

Directions:

> In a bowl, mix the eggs with the paprika, rosemary and the other ingredients, whisk, transfer to a sous vide bag, seal it, introduce in your sous vide machine and cook at 160 degrees F for 30 minutes.

> Divide between plates and serve for breakfast.

Nutrition: calories 200 fat 3 fiber 6 carbs 12 protein 5

Pesto Eggs

Preparation time: 10 minutes

Cooking time: 30 minutes

Servings: 2

Ingredients:

1 tomato, cubed

2 tablespoons basil pesto

4 eggs

Salt and black pepper to the taste

½ teaspoon hot paprika

Directions:

Place the eggs in your sous vide bath, cook at 150 degrees F for 30 minutes and crack them on plates

Divide the pesto, tomato and sprinkle the paprika on each egg and serve for breakfast.

Nutrition: calories 177 fat 3 fiber 6 carbs 8 protein 7

Spinach Scramble

Preparation time: 10 minutes

Cooking time: 20 minutes

Servings: 2

Ingredients:

> ½ teaspoon rosemary, dried
>
> 4 eggs
>
> 1-ounce spinach, chopped
>
> Salt and black pepper to the taste
>
> 1 tablespoon parmesan, grated
>
> 1 tablespoon chives, minced
>
> A pinch of red pepper flakes, crushed

Directions:

> In a bowl, mix eggs with salt, pepper, parmesan and the other ingredients, whisk, pour into a sous vide bag, introduce in your sous vide machine and cook at 140 degrees F for 20 minutes.

Divide between plates and serve for breakfast.

Nutrition: calories 211 fat 3 fiber 6 carbs 8 protein 2

Herbed Ricotta Cheese

Preparation time: 10 minutes

Cooking time: 40 minutes

Servings: 12

Ingredients:

    3 tablespoons chives, chopped

    1 tablespoon oregano, chopped

    1 tablespoon parsley, chopped

    3 quarts almond milk

    1 cup white vinegar

Directions:

Put the milk in a big sous vide bag, remove most of the air, seal, submerge in bath water and cook in your sous vide machine for 40 minutes at 172 degrees F.

Add the vinegar, and the other ingredients, stir, open the bag, collect the curd, drain for a couple of hours and serve for breakfast.

Nutrition: calories 132 fat 3 fiber 3 carbs 7 protein 7

LUNCH

Green Chicken Curry With & Noodles

Preparation Time: 3 hours

Cooking Time: 25-75 minutes

Servings: 2

Ingredients:

1 chicken breast, boneless and skinless

Salt and black pepper to taste

1 can (5 oz coconut milk

2 tbsp green curry paste

1¾ cups chicken stock

1 cup shiitake mushrooms

5 kaffir lime leaves, torn in half

2 tbsp fish sauce

1½ tbsp sugar

½ cup Thai basil leaves, roughly chopped

2 oz cooked egg noodle nests

1 cup cilantro, roughly chopped

1 cup bean sprouts

2 tbsp fried noodles

2 red chilis, roughly chopped

Directions:

Prepare a water bath and place the Sous Vide in it. Set to 138 F. Season the chicken with salt and pepper. Place it in a vacuum-sealable bag. Release air by the water displacement method, seal and submerge the bag in the water bath. Cook for 90 minutes.

Passed 35 minutes, heat a saucepan over medium heat and stir the green curry paste and half coconut milk. Cook for 5-10 minutes until the coconut milk star thicken. Add the chicken stock and the rest of the coconut milk. Cook again for 15 minutes.

Lower the heat and add the kaffir lime leaves, shiitake mushrooms, sugar and fish sauce. Cook for at least 10 minutes. Remove from the heat and add the basil.

Once the timer has stopped, remove the bag and allow cooling for 5 minutes then chop in tiny slices. Serve in a soup bowl the curry sauce, the cooked noodles and the chicken. Top with bean sprouts, cilantro, chilis and fried noodles.

Nutrition: Calories 352, Fat 5, Fiber 3, Carbs 7, Protein 5

Pesto Chicken Mini Bites With Avocado

Preparation Time: 1 hour 40 minutes

Cooking Time: 25-75 minutes

Servings: 2

Ingredients:

1 chicken breast, boneless, skinless, butterflied

Salt and black pepper to taste

1 tbsp sage

3 tbsp olive oil

1 tbsp pesto

1 zucchini, sliced

1 avocado

1 cup fresh basil leaves

Directions:

Prepare a water bath and place the Sous Vide in it. Set to 138 F.

Powder the chicken breast until getting thicken. Season with sage, pepper and salt. Place it in a vacuum-sealable bag. Add 1 tbsp of oil and pesto. Release air by the water displacement method, seal and submerge the bag in the water bath. Cook for 75 minutes. After 60 minutes, heat 1 tbsp of olive oil in a skillet over medium-high heat, add the zucchini and ¼ cup water. Cook until the water has evaporated. Once the timer has stopped, remove the chicken from the bag.

Heat the remaining olive oil in a skillet over medium heat and sear the chicken for 2 minutes per side. Set aside and allow cooling. Chop the chicken in tiny slices like the zucchini. Slice the avocado to the same size. Serve the chicken with slices of avocado on the top. Garnish with zucchini slices and basil.

Nutrition: Calories 352, Fat 5, Fiber 3, Carbs 7, Protein 5

Cheesy Chicken Balls

Preparation Time: 1 hour 15 minutes

Cooking Time: 25-75 minutes

Servings: 6

Ingredients:

1 pound ground chicken

2 tbsp onion, finely chopped

¼ tsp garlic powder

Salt and black pepper to taste

2 tbsp breadcrumbs

1 egg

32 small, diced cubes of mozzarella cheese

1 tbsp butter

3 tbsp panko

½ cup tomato sauce

½ oz grated Pecorino Romano cheese

Chopped parsley

Directions:

Prepare a water bath and place the Sous Vide in it.
Set to 146 F. In a bowl, mix the chicken, onion,
salt, garlic powder, pepper and seasoned

breadcrumbs. Add the egg and combine well. Form 32 medium-size balls and fill with a cube of cheese, make sure the mix covers the cheese well.

Place the balls in a vacuum-sealable bag and let chill for 20 minutes. Then, release air by the water displacement method, seal and submerge the bag in the water bath. Cook for 45 minutes.

Once the timer has stopped, remove the balls. Heat the butter in a skillet over medium-high heat and add the panko. Cook until toast. As well cook the tomato sauce. In a servings dish, place the balls and glaze with the tomato sauce. Top with the panko and cheese. Garnish with parsley.

Nutrition: Calories 352, Fat 5, Fiber 3, Carbs 7, Protein 5

Cheesy Turkey Burgers

Preparation Time: 1 hour 45 minutes

Cooking Time: 25-75 minutes

Servings: 6

Ingredients:

6 tsp olive oil

1½ pounds ground turkey

16 cream crackers, crushed

2½ tbsp chopped fresh parsley

2 tbsp chopped fresh basil

½ tbsp Worcestershire sauce

½ tbsp soy sauce

½ tsp garlic powder

1 egg

6 buns, toasted

6 tomato slices

6 Romaine lettuce leaves

6 slices Monterey Jack cheese

Directions:

Prepare a water bath and place the Sous Vide in it. Set to 148 F. Combine the turkey, crackers, parsley, basil, soy sauce and garlic powder. Add the egg and mix using your hands.

In a baking sheet with wax pepper, with the mixture create 6 patties and place them. Cover it and transfer into the fridge

Remove the patties from the fridge and place it in three vacuum-sealable bag. Release air by the water displacement method, seal and submerge the bag in the water bath. Cook for 1 hour and 15 minutes.

Once the timer has stopped, remove the patties. Discard the cooking juices.

Heat the olive oil in a skillet over high heat and place the patties. Sear for 45 seconds per side. Place the patties over the toasted buns. Top with tomato, lettuce and cheese. Serve.

Nutrition: Calories 352, Fat 5, Fiber 3, Carbs 7, Protein 5

DINNER

Elk Steak

Preparation Time: 10 mins

Cooking Time: 2 hours

Servings: 4

Ingredients:

For Steaks:

4 elk steaks

sea salt, to taste

bacon Fat, as required

For Brussels Sprouts:

3-4 cups brussels sprouts, trimmed

1-2 tablespoons coconut oil

sea salt, to taste

1-2 tablespoons balsamic vinegar

Directions:

Attach the sous vide immersion circulator using an adjustable clamp to a Cambro container or pot filled with water and preheat to 130°F.

Season steaks evenly with salt.

Into a cooking pouch, add the steaks. Seal pouch tightly after squeezing out the excess air. Place pouch in sous vide bath and set the cooking time for 1-2 hours.

Preheat the oven to 400°F.

For the Brussels sprouts: In a pan of boiling water, cook Brussels sprouts for 3 minutes.

Drain well and immediately plunge into a large bowl of ice water to cool.

After cooling, cut Brussels sprouts in half.

Arrange Brussels sprout onto a baking sheet. Top with some coconut oil and sprinkle with salt.

Place baking sheet in oven and bake for 2 minutes.

Remove baking sheet from oven and toss sprouts well.

Bake for a further 20 minutes, tossing once midway.

Remove sprouts from oven and transfer into a bowl with the vinegar, and toss to coat.

Remove steak pouch from sous vide bath and carefully open it. Remove steaks from pouch. With paper towels, pat steaks completely dry.

In a cast iron skillet, heat bacon Fat and sear steaks for 1 minute per side.

Serve steaks alongside Brussels sprouts.

Nutrition: Calories 317 Total Fat 10.6g Total Carb 0.5g Dietary Fiber 0.2g Protein 52.1g

Lamb Steaks

Preparation Time: 10 mins

Cooking Time: 6 hours

Servings: 4

Ingredients:

⅔ cup olive oil, divided as ½ cup and the remaining
oil

4 garlic cloves, crushed

1 sprig thyme

1 sprig rosemary

1 bay leaf

4 x 7-ounce lamb leg steaks

Directions:

In a large bowl, mix together ½ cup of oil, garlic, the
herbs and the bay leaf.

Add steaks to bowl and coat generously with
mixture.

Refrigerate for 1-4 hours.

Attach the sous vide immersion circulator using an
adjustable clamp to a Cambro container or pot
filled with water and preheat to 144°F.

Into a cooking pouch, add steaks and remaining oil. Seal pouch tightly after squeezing out the excess air. Place pouch in sous vide bath and set the cooking time for 6 hours.

Remove pouch from sous vide bath and carefully open it. Remove steaks from pouch. With paper towels, pat steaks completely dry.

Heat a cast iron skillet over high heat, and sear steaks until browned from both sides.

Serve immediately.

Nutrition: Calories 317 Total Fat 10.6g Total Carb 0.5g Dietary Fiber 0.2g Protein 52.1g

Lamb Sweetbreads

Preparation Time: 15 mins

Cooking Time: 45 mins

Servings: 4

Ingredients:

4 cups milk, divided

10 ounces lamb sweetbreads

3 ½ ounces soft flour

1-ounce dried rosemary, crushed

salt and freshly ground black pepper, to taste

oil, as required

Directions:

Into a large bowl, add 2 cups of milk and the lamb
sweetbreads, and allow to soak for 8 hours.

Attach the sous vide immersion circulator using an
adjustable clamp to a Cambro container or pot
filled with water and preheat to 144°F.

Drain lamb sweetbreads.

Into a large pan, add 4 cups of water and bring to a
boil.

Add lamb sweetbreads and cook for 10 seconds.

Remove lamb sweetbreads from boiling water and immediately plunge into a large bowl of ice water to cool.

After cooling, peel off any excess sinew.

Into a cooking pouch, add lamb sweetbreads and the remaining 2 cups of milk. Seal pouch tightly after squeezing out the excess air. Place pouch in sous vide bath and set the cooking time for 40 minutes.

Remove pouch from sous vide bath and carefully open it. Remove lamb sweetbreads from pouch. With paper towels, pat lamb sweetbreads completely dry.

In a bowl, mix together the flour, rosemary, salt and black pepper.

Roll lamb sweetbreads evenly with flour mixture.

In a cast iron pan, heat some oil and fry and pan fry lamb sweetbreads until crisp.

Serve immediately.

Nutrition: Calories 317 Total Fat 10.6g Total Carb 0.5g Dietary Fiber 0.2g Protein 52.1g

Venison Steaks

Preparation Time: 20 mins

Cooking Time: 36 hours

Servings: 4

Ingredients:

For Steaks:

1 x 1-pound venison blade steak

2 shallots, roughly chopped

6 cloves garlic, roughly chopped

3 chili peppers, seeded and roughly chopped

salt and freshly ground black pepper, to taste

1 tablespoon avocado oil

For Gravy:

reserved cooking liquid mixture

2 tablespoons butter

1 teaspoon all-purpose flour

1 cup beef broth

For Garnish:

black mustard blossoms

micro green herbs

red amaranth

Directions:

For the steak:

To a large bowl, add the steak, shallots, garlic, chili peppers, salt, and pepper, and toss to coat well.

Refrigerate for at least 30 minutes.

Attach the sous vide immersion circulator using an adjustable clamp to a Cambro container or pot filled with water and preheat to 137°F.

Into a cooking pouch, add steak mixture. Seal pouch tightly after squeezing out the excess air. Place pouch in sous vide bath and place a weight over pouch. Set the cooking time for 36 hours.

Remove pouch from sous vide bath and carefully open it. Remove steak from pouch, reserving cooking liquid mixture. With paper towels, pat steak completely dry and set aside to rest briefly.

In a skillet, heat 1 tablespoon of avocado oil and sear steak for 1 minute per side.

Transfer steak onto a plate and keep aside.

For the gravy:

In in a food processor, add the reserved cooking liquid mixture and pulse until a smooth paste is formed.

In a heavy-bottomed pan, melt butter. Stir in flour
and paste cook until browned slightly, stirring
continuously.

Reduce heat and stir in paste and broth. Bring to a
boil and remove from heat.

Cut steak into desired slices and decorate with
favorite garnish.

Serve with gravy.

Nutrition: Calories 317 Total Fat 10.6g Total Carb 0.5g
Dietary Fiber 0.2g Protein 52.1g

Rabbit Legs

Preparation Time: 10 mins

Cooking Time: 4 hours

Servings: 4

Ingredients:

- 2 rabbit legs
- 1 teaspoon kosher salt
- ½ teaspoon freshly ground black pepper
- 1 sprig rosemary
- 2 tablespoons extra-virgin olive oil

Directions:

Attach the sous vide immersion circulator using an adjustable clamp to a Cambro container or pot filled with water and preheat to 145°F.

Season rabbit legs with salt and pepper.

Into a cooking pouch, add the rabbit legs, rosemary and olive oil. Seal pouch tightly after squeezing out the excess air. Place pouch in sous vide bath and set the cooking time for 4 hours.

Preheat broiler to high. Line a rimmed baking sheet with a piece of foil.

Remove pouch from sous vide bath and carefully open it. Remove rabbit legs from pouch. With paper towels, pat rabbit legs completely dry.

Arrange rabbit legs onto prepare baking sheet. Broil for 5 minutes.

Serve immediately.

Nutrition: Calories 317 Total Fat 10.6g Total Carb 0.5g Dietary Fiber 0.2g Protein 52.1g

Osso Buco

Preparation Time: 20 mins

Cooking Time: 72 hours 15 mins

Servings: 4

Ingredients:

2 veal shanks

salt and freshly ground black pepper, to taste

flour, as required

extra-virgin olive oil, as required

butter, as required

1 onion, chopped

2 ounces pancetta, chopped

1 glass dry white wine

½ cup concentrated veal broth

2 teaspoons tomato paste

For Gremolata:

fresh flat leaf parsley, as required

1 fresh sprig rosemary

2 fresh sage leaves

fresh lemon zest, as required

1 garlic clove

Directions:

Attach the sous vide immersion circulator using an adjustable clamp to a Cambro container or pot filled with water and preheat to 143°F.

With a sharp knife, make 1-inch cuts in the around the shanks.

With paper towels, pat shanks and season with salt and black pepper.

Dust each shank with flour evenly.

In a frying pan, heat olive oil and sear shanks until browned from both sides.

Transfer shanks onto a plate. Discard most of the oil from the pan.

In the same pan, melt butter and sauté onion until translucent.

Add pancetta and sauté until slightly golden.

Stir in wine and cook until half the wine is absorbed.

Stir in veal broth and tomato paste, then remove from heat.

Into a large cooking ouch, place shanks and wine mixture. Seal pouch tightly after squeezing out the excess air. Place pouch in sous vide bath and set the cooking time for 72 hours.

Meanwhile for gremolata:

in a food processor, add all ingredients listed under gremolata section above, and pulse until minced finely.

Remove pouch from sous vide bath and carefully open it. Remove shanks from pouch.

Transfer shanks with mixture onto serving platter. Top with gremolata and serve.

Nutrition: Calories 317 Total Fat 10.6g Total Carb 0.5g Dietary Fiber 0.2g Protein 52.1g

Rabbit Loin

Preparation Time: 20 mins

Cooking Time: 4 hours

Servings: 4

Ingredients:

6 tablespoons olive oil, divided 4 + 2

1-ounce fresh flat leaf parsley, chopped

½ ounce fresh dill, chopped

2 tablespoons Dijon mustard

1 teaspoon apple cider vinegar

1 teaspoon garlic, minced

½ teaspoon freshly ground black pepper

¼ teaspoon ground ginger

pinch of salt

4 x 8-ounce rabbit loins

Directions:

Attach the sous vide immersion circulator using an adjustable clamp to a Cambro container or pot filled with water and preheat to 150°F.

Into a bowl, add all ingredients except 2 tablespoons of oil and the rabbit loins. Mix well.

Add rabbit loins and coat generously with mixture.

In 4 separate cooking pouches, divide rabbit loins with marinade. Seal pouches tightly after squeezing out the excess air. Place pouches in sous vide bath and set the cooking time for 4 hours.

Remove pouches from sous vide bath and carefully open them. Remove rabbit loins from pouches. With paper towels, pat rabbit loins completely dry.

In a skillet, heat remaining oil and sear the loins until golden brown from both sides.

Nutrition: Calories 317   Total Fat 10.6g   Total Carb 0.5g Dietary Fiber 0.2g Protein 52.1g

MEAT

Beef Stroganoff

Preparation Time: 20 minutes

Cooking Time: 1 hour 20 minutes

Servings: 2

Ingredients:

- 1½ pounds beef loin
- 6 tablespoons unsalted butter
- 1 cup button mushrooms, chopped
- 1 onion, finely chopped
- 3 tablespoons all-purpose flour
- 1 cup beef broth
- 2 tablespoons dry white wine
- 1 cup sour cream
- Rosemary sprigs

Directions:

Preheat your Sous Vide machine to 136 °F.

Season the steaks with salt and pepper and place them in the vacuum bag, putting a piece of butter and rosemary sprigs on top of each steak.

Seal the bag and cook the steaks in the preheated water bath for 1 hour.

In the meantime, heat 2 tablespoons of butter in a skillet and sauté the chopped onion until translucent.

Add the mushrooms, salt, and pepper to taste, and cook until the liquid evaporates. Set aside.

Sear the steaks in 1 tablespoon of butter. Set aside.

Add 2 tablespoons of butter and flour to the pan, mix it well with a spoon, and then add the stock, wine, and cooked mushrooms.

Cook until the sauce thickens. Stir in the sour cream and serve the sauce with the chopped steak over mashed potatoes.

Nutrition: Calories 334, Fat 33, Fiber 3, Carbs 14, Protein 7

Lamb with Basil Chimichurri

Preparation Time: 10 minutes

Cooking Time: 2 hours

Servings: 4

Ingredients:

Lamb chops

12 ounces lamb, frenched

Pepper

Salt

2 cloves garlic, crushed

Basil chimichurri

¼ teaspoon pepper

¼ teaspoon salt

3 tablespoons red wine vinegar

½ tablespoon olive oil

1 teaspoon red chili flakes

2 cloves garlic, minced

1 onion, diced

1 cup fresh basil, finely chopped

Directions:

Set the temperature on your Sous Vide appliance to 133 °F. Season the lamb with pepper and salt, then vacuum seal it together with the crushed garlic and cook for 2 hours.

Meanwhile, combine all basil chimichurri ingredients in a bowl and mix well. Season as desired, then cover and refrigerate to allow the flavors to blend together.

Remove the lamb chops from the vacuum-sealed bag after 2 hours of cooking, and then dry using a paper towel.

Sear with a scalding hot well-oiled pan, and then slice between the bones.

Top liberally with the basil chimichurri sauce. Enjoy!

Nutrition: Calories 334, Fat 33, Fiber 3, Carbs 14, Protein 7

Pork Cheek Ragout

Preparation Time: 30 minutes

Cooking Time: 10 hours

Servings: 8

Ingredients:

2 lbs. skinless pork cheeks

2 finely diced carrots

½ white onion, finely diced

1 cup canned tomato sauce

1 cup canned diced tomatoes

3 sprigs oregano

3 garlic cloves, crushed

1 teaspoon granulated sugar

2 pieces' bay leaves

Kosher salt and black pepper, as needed

Cooked pasta and fresh parsley for servings

Directions:

Prepare the Sous Vide water bath using your immersion circulator and raise the temperature to 180-degrees Fahrenheit.

Add the pork cheeks, carrots, onion, tomato sauce, diced tomatoes, garlic, oregano, sugar, bay leaves, 1 teaspoon of pepper, 1 tablespoon of salt to a heavy-duty re-sealable zip bag.

Seal using the immersion method. Cook for 10 hours.

Once done, remove the bag and then the pork, make sure to reserve the cooking liquid.

Shred using 2 forks into 1-inch pieces, transfer to large bowl and set it to the side.

Remove and discard the oregano from the cooking liquid, pour the contents to a food processor and pulse until the ingredients are uniformly chopped.

Take the sauce and season it well with pepper and salt, pour it over the pork toss to combine.

Toss the pasta with the mixture and serve with parsley!

Nutrition: Calories 334, Fat 33, Fiber 3, Carbs 14, Protein 7

Pork Slices With Noodle Salad

Preparation Time: 20 minutes

Cooking Time: 12 hours

Servings: 2

Ingredients:

- ½ pound boneless pork leg
- 1 tablespoon extra-virgin olive oil
- 1 tablespoon freshly squeezed lime juice
- 1 tablespoon fish sauce
- 1 tablespoon soy sauce
- 1 tablespoon rice vinegar
- 1 tablespoon palm sugar
- 2 vermicelli noodle nests
- ½ thinly sliced scallion
- 2 tablespoons roasted peanuts chopped up
- 2 tablespoons chopped fresh cilantro
- 2 tablespoons chopped fresh mint

Directions:

Prepare the Sous Vide water bath using your immersion circulator and raise the temperature to 176-degrees Fahrenheit.

Add the pork leg to a resealable zip bag alongside the olive oil.

Seal using the immersion method and cook for 12 hours.

Prepare your dressing by mixing the lime juice, soy sauce, fish sauce, rice vinegar, and palm sugar in a small-sized bowl, give the whole mixture a nice stir.

Once cooked, take the pork out from the water bath and allow it to cool.

Shred using forks into bite-sized pieces.

Bring a large pot of water and bring it to a boil over high heat, add the vermicelli noodle and cook for 2-3 minutes.

Transfer to a bowl and add the scallions, mint, cilantro, peanuts, dressing, and pork to the noodle and toss well.

Serve!

Nutrition: Calories 334, Fat 33, Fiber 3, Carbs 14, Protein 7

Pork Chili Verde

Preparation Time: 40 minutes

Cooking Time: 24 hours

Servings: 8

Ingredients:

- 2 lbs. boneless pork shoulder cut up into 1-inch pieces
- 1 tablespoon kosher salt
- 1 tablespoon ground cumin
- 1 teaspoon fresh ground black pepper
- 1 tablespoon extra-virgin olive oil
- 1 lb. tomatillos
- 3 poblano pepper, finely seeded and diced
- ½ white onion finely diced
- 1 jalapeno seeded and diced
- 3 garlic cloves, crushed
- 1 bunch roughly chopped cilantro
- 1 cup chicken broth
- ½ cup fresh squeezed lime juice
- 1 tablespoon Mexican oregano

Directions:

Prepare the Sous Vide water bath using your immersion circulator and raise the temperature to 150-degrees Fahrenheit.

Season the pork with salt, cumin, and pepper.

Take a large skillet and place it over medium-high heat, add the oil and allow it to heat up.

Add the pork and sear for 5-7 minutes.

Increase the heat back to medium-high and add the tomatillos, poblano pepper, onion, jalapeno, and garlic. Cook for 5 minutes until slightly charred.

Transfer the whole prepared mixture to a food processor and add the cilantro, lime juice, chicken broth, oregano, and process for 1 minute.

Transfer the sauce to a resealable zip bag alongside the pork and seal using the immersion method. Submerge it underwater and cook for 24 hours.

Once cooked, remove the bag and transfer the contents to a servings bowl. Sprinkle some salt and pepper and serve over rice.

Nutrition: Calories 334, Fat 33, Fiber 3, Carbs 14, Protein 7

Garlic & Ginger Pork Kebobs

Preparation Time: 30 minutes

Cooking Time: 4 hours

Servings: 4

Ingredients:

- 1 lb. boneless pork shoulder cut up into 1-inch pieces
- 1 tablespoon kosher salt
- 1 tablespoon minced salt
- 1 tablespoon minced fresh ginger
- 1 tablespoon garlic, minced
- 1 teaspoon cumin
- 1 teaspoon coriander
- 1 teaspoon garlic powder
- 1 teaspoon brown sugar
- 1 teaspoon fresh ground black pepper

Directions:

Prepare the Sous Vide water bath using your immersion circulator and raise the temperature to 150-degrees Fahrenheit.

Rub the pork with salt, garlic, ginger, cumin, coriander, garlic powder, pepper, and brown sugar, and transfer to a resealable bag.

Seal using the immersion method and cook for 4 hours.

Heat up the grill to medium-high heat and remove the pork from the bag once cooking is done, pierce it into skewers.

Grill for 3 minutes until browned all around

Serve!

Nutrition: Calories 334, Fat 33, Fiber 3, Carbs 14, Protein 7

Cream-Poached Pork Loin

Preparation Time: 30 minutes

Cooking Time: 4 hours

Servings: 4

Ingredients:

1 – 3 lbs. boneless pork loin roast

Kosher salt and pepper as needed

2 thinly sliced onion

¼ cup cognac

1 cup whole milk

1 cup heavy cream

Directions:

Prepare the Sous Vide water bath using your immersion circulator and raise the temperature to 145-degrees Fahrenheit.

Season the pork with pepper and salt, take a large iron skillet and place it over medium-heat for 5 minutes.

Add the pork and sear for 15 minutes until all sides are browned.

Transfer to a platter, add the onion to the rendered Fat (in the skillet and cook for 5 minutes.

Add the cognac and bring to a simmer. Allow it to cool for 10 minutes.

Add the pork, onion, milk, and cream to a resealable zipper bag and seal using the immersion method. Submerge underwater and cook for 4 hours.

Once cooked, remove the bag from the water and take the pork out, transfer the pork to cutting board and cover it to keep it warm.

Pour the bag contents to a skillet and bring the mixture to a simmer over medium heat, keep cooking for 10 minutes and season with salt and pepper.

Slice the pork and serve with the cream sauce.

Nutrition: Calories 334, Fat 33, Fiber 3, Carbs 14, Protein 7

Hoisin Glazed Pork Tenderloin

Preparation Time: 20 minutes

Cooking Time: 3 hours

Servings: 3

Ingredients:

- 1-piece pork tenderloin, trimmed
- 1 teaspoon kosher salt
- ½ teaspoon freshly ground black pepper
- 3 tablespoons hoisin sauce

Directions:

Prepare the Sous Vide water bath using your immersion circulator and raise the temperature to 145-degrees Fahrenheit.

Take the tenderloins and season it with pepper and salt and transfer to a resealable zip bag.

Seal using the immersion method and cook for 3 hours.

Remove the bag and then the pork, brush with hoisin sauce.

Heat up your grill to high grill and add the tenderloin, sear for 5 minutes until all sides are caramelized.

Allow it to rest and slice the tenderloin into medallions, serve!

Nutrition: Calories 334, Fat 33, Fiber 3, Carbs 14, Protein 7

Smoked Sausage & Cabbage Potatoes

Preparation Time: 25 minutes

Cooking Time: 2 hours

Servings: 4

Ingredients:

- ½ head green cabbage, cored and thinly sliced
- 1 Granny smith apple, peeled and cored, cut up into small dices
- 24 oz. red potatoes cut up into quarters and into ¼ inch thick wedges
- 1 small onion thinly sliced
- ¼ teaspoon celery salt
- 2 tablespoons cider vinegar
- 2 tablespoons packed brown sugar
- Salt and black pepper, as needed
- 1 pound precooked smoked pork sausage sliced up into 4 portions with each portion sliced into half lengthwise
- ½ cup chicken broth
- 2 tablespoons unsalted butter

Directions:

Prepare the Sous Vide water bath using your immersion circulator and raise the temperature to 185-degrees Fahrenheit.

Take a large bowl and add the cabbage, potatoes, onion, apple, cider vinegar, brown sugar, and celery salt. Season with salt and pepper

Divide the mixture and sausage among 2 resealable zip bags and add ¼ cup of chicken broth to each bags.

Seal using the immersion method and cook for 2 hours.

Take a skillet and place it over medium-high heat and add 1 tablespoon of butter, heat it up and add the bag contents to the skillet.

Bring it to a boil and reduce the heat, cook until the liquid evaporates. It should take about 5-6 minutes for the onion, potatoes, cabbage to be browned.

Transfer to a servings platter and repeat the process with the remaining cabbage- sausage mix.

Serve!

Nutrition: Calories 334, Fat 33, Fiber 3, Carbs 14, Protein 7

Boneless Pork Ribs

Preparation Time: 30 minutes

Cooking Time: 8 hours

Servings: 4

Ingredients:

- 1/3 cup unsweetened coconut milk
- 2 tablespoons peanut butter
- 2 tablespoons soy sauce
- 2 tablespoons light brown sugar
- 2 tablespoons dry white wine
- 2-inch fresh lemongrass
- 1 tablespoon Sriracha sauce
- 1 inch peeled fresh ginger
- 2 garlic cloves
- 2 teaspoons sesame oil
- 12 oz. boneless country style pork ribs
- Chopped up fresh cilantro and steamed basmati rice for servings

Directions:

Prepare the Sous Vide water bath using your immersion circulator and increase the temperature to 134-degrees Fahrenheit.

Add the coconut milk, peanut butter, soy sauce, brown sugar, wine, lemongrass, ginger, Sriracha sauce, sesame oil and garlic to a blender, blend until smooth.

Add the ribs to a resealable zip bag alongside the sauce and seal using the immersion method. Cook for 8 hours.

Once done, remove the bag and take the ribs out from the bag, transfer to plate.

Pour the bag contents to a large skillet and place it over medium-high heat, bring to a boil and lower heat to medium-low. Simmer for 10-15 minutes.

Then, add the ribs to the sauce and turn well to coat it.

Simmer for 5 minutes.

Garnish with fresh cilantro and serve with the rice!

Nutrition: Calories 334, Fat 33, Fiber 3, Carbs 14, Protein 7

Coffee-Chili Pork Porterhouse

Preparation Time: 20 minutes

Cooking Time: 2 hours 30 minutes

Servings: 4

Ingredients:

- 2 pieces bone-in pork porterhouse
- 1 tablespoon ancho chilis powder
- 1 tablespoon ground coffee
- 1 tablespoon light brown sugar
- 1 tablespoon garlic salt
- 1 tablespoon extra-virgin olive oil

Directions:

Prepare your Sous Vide water bath using your immersion circulator and increase the temperature to 145-degrees Fahrenheit.

Add the pork to a resealable bag and seal using the immersion method. Cook for 2 ½ hours.

Make your seasoning mixture by adding the chili powder, coffee, brown sugar, and garlic salt to a small bowl.

Remove the bag. Then take the pork out from the bag, pat it dry using kitchen towel.

Rub the chop with seasoning.

Take a cast iron skillet and put it over high heat and add the olive oil and sear the pork for 1-2 minutes per side.

Once done, transfer the pork to a cutting board and allow it to rest for 5 minutes, slice and serve!

Nutrition: Calories 334, Fat 33, Fiber 3, Carbs 14, Protein 7

Balsamic Glazed Pork Rib Chop

Preparation Time: 20 minutes

Cooking Time: 180 minutes

Servings: 2

Ingredients:

    1-piece bone-in pork chop
    Kosher salt and black pepper, as needed
    1 tablespoon extra-virgin olive oil
    4 tablespoons aged balsamic vinegar

Directions:

Prepare your Sous Vide water bath using your immersion circulator and increase the temperature to 145-degrees Fahrenheit.

Take the pork and carefully season it with pepper and salt, transfer to a resealable zipper bag and seal using the immersion method.

Cook for 3 hours and remove the bag from the water bath and then the pork and pat it dry.

Take a sauté pan and place it over high heat for 5 minutes, add the olive oil and the pork chops.

Sear until browned on both sides.

Add 3 tablespoons of balsamic vinegar to the skillet and bring to a rapid simmer, keep simmer while spooning the vinegar over the chop. Keep repeating for 1 minute.

Once done, transfer the dish to your servings plate and serve it with the rest of the balsamic.

Nutrition: Calories 334, Fat 33, Fiber 3, Carbs 14, Protein 7

FISH & SEAFOOD

Herbed Pork and Sun-dried Tomatoes

Preparation Time: 10 minutes

Cooking Time: 2 hours

Servings: 2

Ingredients:

2 pounds pork roast, sliced

1 cup sun-dried tomatoes, chopped

2 tablespoons olive oil

Juice of 1 lime

1 tablespoon mustard

Zest of 1 lime, grated

½ teaspoon cloves, crushed

1 teaspoon oregano, dried

1 teaspoon coriander, ground

1 teaspoon thyme, chopped

1 tablespoon chives, chopped

Directions:

In a large sous vide bag, combine the roast with the tomatoes, oil and the other ingredients, seal the bag, submerge in the sous vide machine and cook at 180 degrees F for 2 hours

Divide between plates and serve right away.

Nutrition: Calories 336, Fat 6, Fiber 6, Carbs 16, Protein 5

Buttery Pork Tenderloin

Preparation Time: 10 minutes

Cooking Time: 2 hours

Servings: 4

Ingredients:

2 pounds pork tenderloin, sliced

½ teaspoon turmeric powder

1 teaspoon chili powder

Juice of 1 lime

1 and ½ tablespoons Italian seasoning

Salt and black pepper to the taste

2 tablespoons butter, melted

Directions:

In a sous vide bag, combine the pork with the melted butter and the other ingredients, seal the bag, introduce it in the preheated water oven and cook at 135 degrees F for 2 hours.

Divide between plates and serve with a side salad.

Nutrition: Calories 321, Fat 4, Fiber 7, Carbs 12, Protein 5

Garlic and Nutmeg Pork

Preparation Time: 10 minutes

Cooking Time: 2 hours

Servings:

Ingredients:

2 pounds pork roast, sliced

4 garlic cloves, minced

1 teaspoon nutmeg, ground

2 tablespoons olive oil

Juice of 1 lime

Salt and black pepper to the taste

1 teaspoon rosemary, dried

2 bay leaves

1 tablespoon cilantro, chopped

Directions:

In a sous vide bag, combine the pork with the garlic, nutmeg and the other ingredients, seal, introduce them into your preheated water oven and cook at 180 degrees F for 2 hours.

Divide between plates and serve.

Nutrition: Calories 353, Fat 7, Fiber 8, Carbs 15, Protein 17

Salmon Gravlax

Preparation Time: 30 minutes

Cooking Time: 1 Hour

Servings: 8

Ingredients:

8 salmon fillets

4 tbsp sugar

4 tbsp salt

Directions:

Preheat your cooking machine to 104 degrees F.

In a small bowl, mix the sugar with salt.

Season the salmon with the mixture and set aside for half an hour.

Rinse the salmon fillets and place them into the vacuum bag.

Seal it, setting the timer for 1 hour.

Serve immediately with toasted bread and cream cheese.

Nutrition: Calories: 260 Protein: 35 g Fats: 11 g Carbs: 7 g

Salmon Teriyaki

Preparation Time: 30 minutes

Cooking Time: 1 Hour

Servings: 8

Ingredients:

8 salmon fillets

8 tbsp Teriyaki sauce

Directions:

Preheat your cooking machine to 104 degrees F.

Evenly cover the salmon fillets with the Teriyaki
sauce set aside for half an hour.

Place the fillets in the vacuum bag.

Seal it, setting the timer for 1 hour.

Serve immediately with steamed white rice.

Nutrition: Calories: 277 Protein: 35 g Fats:5 g Carbs:
9 g

Ginger Salmon

Preparation Time: 1 Hour

Cooking Time: 40 minutes

Servings: 2

Ingredients:

2 salmon fillets

2 tbsp soy sauce

1 tbsp liquid honey

1 tbsp sesame oil

1 tbsp ginger root, minced

Chili pepper to taste

Directions:

Put all ingredients into the vacuum bag and set aside for 1 hour to marinate.

In the meantime, preheat the water bath to 125 degrees F.

Seal the bag and set the timer for 30 minutes.

When the time is up, you can serve salmon immediately, or sear it on both sides in a cast iron skillet until it browns a bit and then serve over rice, pouring the juices from the bag over the rice.

Nutrition: Calories: 277 Protein: 35 g Fats: 5 g Carbs: 9 g

POULTRY

Chicken & Melted Leeks

Preparation Time: 15 minutes

Cooking Time: 45 minutes

Servings: 4

Ingredients:

4 x 6 oz. skinless chicken breast

Salt and pepper as needed

3 tablespoons butter

1 large leek, cleaned and sliced crossways

½ cup panko

2 tablespoons chopped parsley

1 oz. cheddar cheese

1 tablespoon olive oil

Directions:

Prepare your water bath using your Sous Vide immersion circulator and raise the temperature to 145-degrees Fahrenheit

Take the chicken breast and season it generously on both sides with salt and pepper and put in a zip bag

Seal using the immersion method and cook for 45 minutes

Take a skillet and add 2 tablespoon of butter over medium heat, allow the butter to heat up and add the leeks

Stir to coat them

Season with salt and pepper

Then, lower down the heat to low and cook for additional 10 minutes

Put a clean skillet over a medium heat. Put in a tablespoon of butter

Add the panko and toast, and stir well until the panko is hot

Spoon the panko mixture from the skillet into a separate bowl and add the cheddar cheese and chopped up parsley, mix well

Once the chicken breasts are thoroughly cooked, remove them from the bag and pat dry

Heat the olive oil over a high heat and sear the breasts for 1 minute

Serve each breast on the melted leek, and top with the toasted panko/cheese mix

Nutrition: Calories: 803 Carbohydrate: 11g Protein: 51g Fat: 61g Sugar: 3g Sodium: 323mg

Moroccan Chicken Meal

Preparation Time: 15 minutes

Cooking Time: 60 minutes

Servings: 2

Ingredients:

- 6 chicken tenderloin
- 4 cups pumpkin, cut into cubes and roasted
- 4 cups rocket lettuce
- 4 tablespoons sliced almonds
- Juice of 1 lemon
- 2 tablespoons olive oil
- 4 tablespoons red onion, chopped
- 2 pinches paprika
- 2 pinches turmeric
- 2 pinches cumin
- 2 pinches salt

Directions:

Prepare your water bath using your Sous Vide immersion circulator, and raise the temperature to 140-degrees Fahrenheit

Put the chicken and the seasoning in a heavy-duty, resealable bag

Seal it using the immersion/water displacement method

Submerge the bag and let it cook for about 60 minutes

Once done, take the chicken out from the bag and sear the tenderloins in a very hot pan, allowing 1 minute per side

Put all the remaining ingredients in a serving bowl and toss them well

Cover the chicken with your salad and serve!

Nutrition: Calories: 304 Carbohydrate: 34g Protein: 22g Fat: 9g Sugar: 7g Sodium: 529mg

Chicken Breast Meal

Preparation Time: 5 minutes

Cooking Time: 60 minutes

Servings: 2

Ingredients:

1-piece boneless chicken breast

Salt and pepper as needed

Garlic powder as needed

Directions:

Prepare your water bath using your Sous Vide immersion circulator, and increase the temperature to 150-degrees Fahrenheit

Carefully drain the chicken breast and pat dry using a kitchen towel

Season the breast with garlic powder, pepper and salt

Place in a resealable bag and seal using the immersion method

Submerge and cook for 1 hour

Serve!

Nutrition: Calories: 150 Carbohydrate: 0g Protein: 18g Fat: 8g Sugar: 0g Sodium: 257mg

Chicken Stew with Mushrooms

Preparation Time: 1 hour 5 minutes

Cooking Time: 50-120 minutes

Servings: 2

Ingredients:

2 medium-sized chicken thighs, skinless

½ cup fire-roasted tomatoes, diced

½ cup chicken stock

1 tbsp tomato paste

½ cup button mushrooms, chopped

1 medium-sized celery stalk

1 small carrot, chopped

1 small onion, chopped

1 tbsp fresh basil, finely chopped

1 garlic clove, crushed

Salt and black pepper to taste

Directions:

Make a water bath, place Sous Vide in it, and set to 129 F. Rub the thighs with salt and pepper. Set aside. Chop the celery stalk into half-inch long pieces.

Now, place the meat in a large vacuum-sealable bag along with onion, carrot, mushrooms, celery stalk, and fire roasted tomatoes. Submerge the sealed bag in the water bath and set the timer for 45 minutes.

Once the timer has stopped, remove the bag from the water bath and open it. The meat should be falling off the bone easily, so remove the bones.

Heat up some oil in a medium-sized saucepan and add garlic. Briefly fry – for about 3 minutes, stirring constantly. Add the contents of the bag, chicken stock, and tomato paste. Bring it to a boil and reduce the heat to medium. Cook for 5 more minutes, stirring occasionally. Serve sprinkled with the basil.

Nutrition: Calories: 150 Carbohydrate: 0g Protein: 18g Fat: 8g Sugar: 0g Sodium: 257mg

Easiest No-Sear Chicken Breast

Preparation Time: 75 minutes

Cooking Time: 50-120 minutes

Servings: 3

Ingredients:

1 lb. chicken breasts, boneless

Salt and black pepper to taste

1 tsp garlic powder

Directions:

Make a water bath, place Sous Vide in it, and set it to 150 F. Pat dry the chicken breasts and season with salt, garlic powder, and pepper. Put the chicken in a vacuum-sealable bag, release air by the water displacement method and seal it.

Place it in the water and set the timer to cook for 1 hour. Once the timer has stopped, remove and unseal the bag. Remove the chicken and chill it for later use.

Nutrition: Calories: 150 Carbohydrate: 0g Protein: 18g Fat: 8g Sugar: 0g Sodium: 257mg

Orange Chicken Thighs

Preparation Time: 2 hours

Cooking Time: 50-120 minutes

Servings: 4

Ingredients:

2 pounds chicken thighs

2 small chili peppers, finely chopped

1 cup chicken broths

1 onion, chopped

½ cup freshly squeezed orange juice

1 tsp orange extract, liquid

2 tbsp vegetable oil

1 tsp barbecue seasoning mix

Fresh parsley to garnish

Directions:

Make a water bath, place Sous Vide in it, and set to
167 F.

Heat up the olive oil in a large saucepan.

Add chopped onions and stir-fry for 3 minutes, over
a medium temperature – until translucent.

In a food processor, combine the orange juice with chili pepper, and orange extract.

Pulse until well combined.

Pour the mixture into a saucepan and reduce the heat. Simmer for 10 minutes.

Coat chicken with barbecue seasoning mix and place in a saucepan.

Add in chicken broth and cook until half of the liquid evaporates.

Remove to a large vacuum-sealable bag and seal. Submerge the bag in the water bath and cook for 45 minutes.

Once the timer has stopped, remove the bag from the water bath and open it.

Garnish with fresh parsley and serve.

Nutrition: Calories: 150 Carbohydrate: 0g Protein: 18g Fat: 8g Sugar: 0g Sodium: 257mg

Thyme Chicken with Lemon

Preparation Time: 2 hours 15 minutes

Cooking Time: 50-120 minutes

Servings: 3

Ingredients:

3 chicken thighs

Salt and black pepper to taste

3 slices lemon

3 sprigs thyme

3 tbsp olive oil for searing

Directions:

Make a water bath, place Sous Vide in it, and set to
165 F.

Season the chicken with salt and pepper. Top with
lemon slices and thyme sprigs.

Place them in a vacuum-sealable bag, release air by
the water displacement method and seal the bag.

Submerge the bag in the water bag and set the timer
for 2 hours.

Once the timer has stopped, remove and unseal the
bag.

Heat olive oil in a cast iron pan over high heat.

Place the chicken thighs, skin down in the skillet and sear until golden brown.

Garnish with extra lemon wedges. Serve with a side of cauli rice.

Nutrition: Calories: 150 Carbohydrate: 0g Protein: 18g Fat: 8g Sugar: 0g Sodium: 257mg

Pepper Chicken Salad

Preparation Time: 1 hour 15 minutes

Cooking Time: 50-120 minutes

Servings: 4

Ingredients:

4 chicken breasts, boneless and skinless

¼ cup vegetable oil plus three tbsp for salad

1 medium-sized onion, peeled and finely chopped

6 cherry tomatoes, halved

Salt and black pepper to taste

1 cup lettuce, finely chopped

2 tbsp of freshly squeezed lemon juice

Directions:

Make a water bath, place Sous Vide in it, and set to 149 F.

Thoroughly rinse the meat under the cold water and pat dry using a kitchen paper.

Cut the meat into bite-sized pieces and place in a vacuum-sealable bag along with ¼ cup of oil and seal.

Submerge the bag in the water bath.

Once the timer has stopped, remove the chicken from the bag, pat dry and chill to a room temperature.

In a large bowl mix the onion, tomatoes, and lettuce.

Finally, add the chicken breasts and season with three tablespoons of oil, lemon juice, and some salt to taste.

Top with Greek yogurt and olives. However, it's optional.

Serve cold.

Nutrition: Calories: 150 Carbohydrate: 0g Protein: 18g Fat: 8g Sugar: 0g Sodium: 257mg

Whole Chicken

Preparation Time: 7 hours 15 minutes

Cooking Time: 50-120 minutes

Servings: 6

Ingredients:

- 1 (5 lb.) full chicken, trussed
- 5 cups chicken stock
- 3 cups mixed bell peppers, diced
- 3 cups celery, diced
- 3 cups leeks, diced
- 1 ¼ tsp salt
- 1 ¼ tsp black peppercorns
- 2 Bay leaves

Directions:

Make a water bath, place Sous Vide in it, and set to 150 F. Season the chicken with salt.

Place all the listed ingredients and chicken in a sizable vacuum-sealable bag.

Release air by the water displacement method and seal the vacuum bag.

Drop the bag in water bath and set the timer for 7 hours.

Cover the water with a plastic bag to reduce evaporation and water every 2 hours to the bath.

Once the timer has stopped, remove and unseal the bag.

Preheat a broiler, carefully remove the chicken and pat it dry.

Place the chicken in the broiler and broil it until the skin is golden brown.

Rest the chicken for 8 minutes,

Slice and serve.

Nutrition: Calories: 150 Carbohydrate: 0g Protein: 18g Fat: 8g Sugar: 0g Sodium: 257mg

Simple Spicy Chicken Thighs

Preparation Time: 2 hours 55 minutes

Cooking Time: 50-120 minutes

Servings: 6

Ingredients:

1 lb. chicken thighs, bone-in

3 tbsp butter

1 tbsp cayenne pepper

Salt to taste

Directions:

Make a water bath, place Sous Vide in it, and set to
165 F.

Season the chicken with pepper and salt.

Place chicken with one tablespoon of butter in a
vacuum-sealable bag.

Release air by the water displacement method, seal
and submerge the bag in the water bath.

Set the timer for 2 hours 30 minutes.

Once the timer has stopped, remove the bag and
unseal it.

Preheat a grill and melt the remaining butter in a microwave.

Oil the grill grate with some of the butter and brush the chicken with the remaining butter.

Sear until dark brown color is achieved.

Serve as a snack.

Nutrition: Calories: 150 Carbohydrate: 0g Protein: 18g Fat: 8g Sugar: 0g Sodium: 257mg

SNACKS & DESSERTS

Parsley Cauliflower

Preparation time: 10 minutes

Cooking time: 2 hours

Servings: 4

Ingredients:

- 2 pounds cauliflower florets
- 1 tablespoon lemon juice
- 1 tablespoon lemon zest, grated
- Salt and black pepper to the taste
- 1 tablespoon parsley, chopped
- 3 tablespoons olive oil
- 2 tablespoons soy sauce

Directions:

In a sous vide bag, combine the cauliflower with the lemon juice and the other ingredients, toss, seal, introduce in the preheated water oven and cook at 180 degrees F for 2 hours.

Divide between plates and serve.

Nutrition: calories 128 fat 2 fiber 3 carbs 7 protein 6

Mushroom and Broccoli Mix

Preparation time: 10 minutes

Cooking time: 1 hour

Servings: 4

Ingredients:

2 tablespoons olive oil

Salt and black pepper to the taste

2 garlic cloves, minced

A handful parsley, chopped

1 pound broccoli florets

½ pound white mushrooms, halved

2 tablespoons balsamic vinegar

Directions:

In a sous vide bag, combine the broccoli with the mushrooms, vinegar and the other ingredients, toss, seal the bag, introduce in your preheated water bag and cook at 175 degrees F for 1 hour.

Divide between plates and serve.

Nutrition: calories 160 fat 4 fiber 6 carbs 2 protein 12

Cumin Okra

Preparation time: 10 minutes

Cooking time: 40 minutes

Servings: 4

Ingredients:

1 tablespoon balsamic vinegar

Salt and black pepper to the taste

1 tablespoon chives, chopped

1 pound okra, sliced

2 tablespoons olive oil

1 red onion, sliced

Directions:

In a sous vide bag, combine the okra with the oil and the other ingredients, toss, seal the bag, submerge in the preheated water oven and cook at 180 degrees F for 40 minutes.

Divide between plates and serve as a side dish.

Nutrition: calories 170 fat 2 fiber 3 carbs 12 protein 6

Okra Mix and Eggplant

Preparation time: 10 minutes

Cooking time: 1 hour

Servings: 4

Ingredients:

   1 tablespoon red wine vinegar

   ½ teaspoon coriander, ground

   ½ teaspoon cumin, ground

   Salt and black pepper to the taste

   ¼ cup chives, chopped

   1 pound eggplant, sliced into thin rounds

   ½ pound okra, sliced

   1 tablespoon olive oil

   1 tablespoon lemon zest, grated

Directions:

   In a sous vide bag, combine the eggplant with the
      okra, oil and the other ingredients, toss, seal the

bag, submerge in the preheated water oven and cook at 183 degrees F for 1 hour.

Divide between plates and serve.

Nutrition: calories 105 fat 1 fiber 1 carbs 6 protein 7

Lemony Okra

Preparation time: 10 minutes

Cooking time: 30 minutes

Servings: 4

Ingredients:

Salt and black pepper to the taste

¼ cup almonds, blanched

2 tablespoons chives, chopped

½ teaspoon turmeric powder

1 pound okra, sliced

Juice of 1 lemon

Zest of 1 lemon, grated

Directions:

In a sous vide bag, combine the okra with the lemon juice, zest and the other ingredients, seal the bag, introduce it in the preheated water oven and cook at 180 degrees F for 30 minutes.

Divide the mix between plates and serve as a side dish.

Nutrition: calories 170 fat 15 fiber 4 carbs 7 protein 4

Cheesy Broccoli

Preparation time: 10 minutes

Cooking time: 1 hour

Servings: 4

Ingredients:

   1 teaspoon chili powder

   1 teaspoon cumin, ground

   1 tablespoon goat cheese, crumbled

   Salt and black pepper to the taste

   3 tablespoons olive oil

   1 pound broccoli florets

   1 garlic clove, minced

Directions:

   In a sous vide bag, combine the broccoli with the garlic, chili and the other ingredients except the cheese, seal the bag, submerge in the preheated water oven and cook at 180 degrees F for 1 hour.

Divide broccoli between plates, sprinkle cheese all over and serve as a side dish.

Nutrition: calories 173 fat 14 fiber 3 carbs 6 protein 5

Lightning Source UK Ltd.
Milton Keynes UK
UKHW021425310521
384684UK00002B/520

9 781803 040554